cul-de-sac rabbits

jax bulstrode

cul-de-sac rabbits

jax bulstrode

MOONRISE

Gubbi Gubbi Country

Australia

Copyright © 2024 Jax Bulstrode

All rights reserved. No part of this book may be reprinted or reproduced or utilised in any form or by any electronic, mechanical, or other means, now known or hereafter invented, including photocopying and recording, or in any information storage or retrieval system, without permission in writing from the publisher.

ISBN 978-0-6459852-5-2

Editor
Wallea Eaglehawk

Copy editor
Sarah Bradbury

Marketing & publishing support
Emma Mitchell
Pooja Kumar
Michelle Bùi Hoàng

Cover art and design by Cat McNicholl

First published in 2024

Moonrise
Gubbi Gubbi Country, Australia
www.moonrise.revolutionaries.com.au

Contents

Land

You can't swim and..02

I still don't have a name for all of this......................03

All at once...05

Seasons through the kitchen window.....................06

It all leads to the end...08

Fire rating...10

Earth signifier...11

Sideoftheroadbeing..13

What is prayer, if not...16

Window shopping in battery point.........................18

Into the heart of tasmania......................................19

My favourite smell is the rain.................................21

God..22

Identity

The truth	26
Shadow time	28
Don't wake me up	29
Cul-de-sac rabbits	30
Poem to myself	32
I change in a dark room	33
Inking	34
Boy who cried wolf was never a goal of mine	35
I bruise here	37
Cornflower blue	40
Boxing day	41
I don't dance and yet	42
The thing I am now	43
How close can you come to owning eternity?	44
Ode in agriculture class	45
Summer shame	46
A perfect day	48
Suburbia	49
Generational girlhood	50
The women in my family	52
And my father	54
You are a good ocean	55
Journal entry no.43	57

Everyone is sad on their birthday......59
Meditations......60
My practice......61
Tell me how we learn to start again......63
I never wanted a gender anyway......64
For when I can't recognise my own face......65
A love letter to:......68
I'll be a shadow of a teen girl until you tell me I don't have to be......72
After dinner......75
Burnt incense......76
I take the number one tram to the end of the line..77
In a violet haze......79
At least I know......80

Love

A safe corner..84

I was and then I wasn't..................................86

Eclipse..87

The olive theory..88

I don't remember my home phone number and....89

You sing through the bedroom door...................90

Tell me about your dream............................92

In this sharehouse..93

This is a funny poem...................................94

If they ask me how I know I will tell them that my friends taught me..95

Picture it..97

I once said I didn't write love poems.............99

According to a new study............................101

The work..102

I'm still scared of space...............................103

I am cosmically insignificant but still so big and so deserving of love......................................104

Body

Today I brush my teeth ... 108
When the fog mist clears ... 110
Body work ... 111
What if I get sick? ... 112
I leave the hospital and the sickness comes with me ... 115
I am brave enough to take care of my body ... 117
In sun and sickness ... 118
Pith cowboy ... 119
Heavyweight champion of forgetting to release the breath ... 120
Time well spent ... 121
An ode to my shadow ... 122
I give the poem time ... 123
You have so many parts of me to meet ... 124
I believe in this ... 125
Year 24 ... 126
Found objects ... 127
Incense balanced on the pizza box ... 128
Yes ... 130
Love letter to the sun ... 131
After ... 132
Sweet dreams ... 133

Acknowledgement

I acknowledge the traditional custodians of the lands on which this book was written, the Boon Wurrung / Bunurong people of the Kulin Nation. I pay my respects to ancestors and Elders, past and present. Without their knowledge and care for this land, these poems would not exist.

"I said to the sun, 'Tell me about the big bang.' The sun said, 'it hurts to become.'"
— Andrea Gibson

"I am out with lanterns, looking for myself."
— Emily Dickinson

Land

You can't swim and

I live in [unresolved]
I do not land

magnesium swimming pool
$4 entry

I can't be loved like this

chlorine and artificial

in public

how do I name
this hunger

the space
between
floating

and anchor

I still don't have a name for all of this

the clouds make me want to cry. they always have. sunsets too. most mangoes. the sound of rain when I am in bed. a deep breath can bring me to sob and if I hug you for another 10 seconds I could weep.

I am notoriously a good listener. I know just the right face to make, mirror your blinks and inhales. you think you see something in me that no one else does. I am a mirror.

I missed approximately 2 years of primary school because I refused to leave the house. and now I can't do my times tables or read a clock. a doctor puts a blanket over my head and tells me to pretend to be a small animal, breaking out of an egg. I walk every cross-country race.

I don't go to church anymore but I do go to choir and I think that might be the same thing. I find the spirit in the library, on the bus, and in my love's hands.

I once had a dog who was too big to sit on my lap. we

left the country and he went grey.

I ask myself where does time slow?

I look for all the places where I am the same. I took a picture.

All at once

You are startled awake
in the middle of the night
the milky moon has fallen
but in the kitchen
there is another light
floating
a pearlescent sphere
that glimmers like a sign
you follow it
open your mouth
and whisper
your silver dream

Seasons through the kitchen window

the tree gives me mangoes
I thumb them open slow
over the kitchen sink

thank the land for this medicine
pray to the dusty sun
and the coming mist

I am too sad today to bear witness
to the shifting of seasons
to the new leaves unfurling
instead, I mourn what was

eucalypt trees once tall lined my street
the bay clear and cobalt
free land not cement smothered

the sky is now not golden
but grey blurred
I hear the birds arriving home,
finding safety and warmth amongst
the seaberry saltbush and coastal wattle

I watch the changing of it all
through the cobwebbed kitchen window

It all leads to the end

we begin
trickling and growing
pooling and spreading

tomorrow morning
we wake to the plague
a kind we are expecting but still
comes as a surprise
unwelcomed
we never learn our lessons
shadows always repeat

thirst is a memory
we danced on the forest fires
smell redgum and acacia ash

salt rains down just like that
our turn is over just as we suspected

bone	turns to	roots
flesh	becomes	dirt

fingernails and scars are just
lightning strikes
and dead leaves

there are no more countdowns
no more calendar clocks
only days
until we sleep in glass coffins
rejoin the mud
ankle-deep and rancid
rub the salt in the ground
and decide we are done with the trees

Fire rating

I opened my eyes to
a grassfire in another country
and sheets bunched around my knees

a natural disaster
left corridors of dust
on unfamiliar highways

I couldn't be angry

I turned the tv off

Earth signifier

coffin woman tempered glass tube
the whole earth prepares to swallow

a young face   who knows the truth
was it a sad   death?

this body   alone
                 watched by the world

the world   which is to say
                 the dirt
                 gravel
                 boot crunched twigs
                 and worms

the point   has changed
this bitter   silence
                 a deep sigh

they   (us)
have   forgotten
              what she looked like
              dancing

eyes   bright

smiling   alive

Sideoftheroadbeing

I am in the night space
in between a broken phone line
and the creek
rushing and cracking
just a sideoftheroad being

but I am at home
only half lit by a
foggy flash of headlight
sunk down into
the gravel and mushed bank
mud in my shoes

this is what I want
for the passing by cars
to recognise me
as the river
as the whole thing
running alongside them
carrying on into the dark
in the morning
when the sun burns away

I get up
stretch my tender bruised knees
and carry myself home to bed
to wake and become

the thing the world
wants to see

believes I am

when I wake
I go to work
with a constant shiver
cold river running
through my blood

in the end
I always return
with the dusk
to the side of the road
to my fear
and the crickets
under my toes
two feet in the water

it is always the same

I swim until the morning
and tell myself
this is what I cannot be

What is prayer, if not

a september morning
gracing us
fresh moment of new

a song sung in the early mist / of birth / of lightness
/ of quiet

these are my hymns
pastoral prayers
sent only to
        the branches soft
        grass bruised knees
        water existing
        untouched valleys
        the first dawn
        a summer shower

these moments
knit together the earth
create my own
practise

this is my congregation
amongst the bugs but
beneath outstretched sky
and within everything else

existing

Window shopping in battery point

and I think I will choose the pink house
puppets in the window and
seashells at the front door
a home built on the top of the hill

I'll plant
heartberry bush, red azolla, a banksia rose

take long walks
down to the bay, past princes park
stop to take in the komerabi
stop to take a photo to show you
when I get back home

Into the heart of tasmania

>*before*
>the first stage was over
>the flat fields
>cutting the gaps
>taunting
>like an early morning
>dream

>*during*
>by the light of the moon
>bulbs of daffodil
>returned
>upon the earth
>how bright
>the garden breathed
>a web of magic

now

we want the same
the warm and slow
take it all in
quiet valley
the yellow of the wattle
hidden behind trees
is a happy sense
I reach for

My favourite smell is the rain

the water in my body
is just visiting

last week
it was a rainstorm
soon it will be
frost on your breath
one day again
return to tears
on my cheeks

we are cyclical after all

the fog leaves your head
only to settle
on the small of my tongue

giving and giving itself
back to me

God

I believe in the earth
in the medicine
of rushing water
too much to
hold a grudge
against she
who pulls the sun
and cleans
with monsoon rains

Identity

The truth

bordering honesty
temples rise
from the bottom of my roots

in the end even the
liars wandered, found the way
continued their walking

all this truth taught me to commit
to the early metal taste between my teeth
taught me to crave the jump
and the drop and the goosebumps
opened the door

again and again
calculating the probabilities
can only warn the thing
won't small it away

tonight, under the covers
beneath the winter rust
this curled up thing

I will hold my own
squeeze just to know

myself real
myself real

Shadow time

does this count as a shadow?

to know you are young,
and act like it

to lay in the shine all day
and not wonder

but also,
to feel the time
ahead of you

sometimes I can't help but try
and count the minutes down

to what
I am not sure

I am just trying to be ready
for
something

Don't wake me up

September is too big, unwelcomed

I do not wish to be in it or have to continue yet

I will claw through to find the joy

Cul-de-sac rabbits

underneath a fingernail moon
I crawl to the tub
turn the faucet too hot
and soak in orange peels
whisper to my knees

this is my favourite
kind of liminal space
waiting
on purpose

two palms faced up
renaming myself
nowhere child

for now
I am stuck with
the cul-de-sac rabbits
in sleepwalk suburbs

I have been here a hundred times

I'll wait right here for you to find me

Poem to myself
after Joseph Fasano

no one knows the dog that waits in me
no one knows my heart is a shy boy
I carry through the water toward the sun
no one knows the way I softly want
but I do
I do
I will wake today and lift my hands
I will walk today and whisper the truth
I will sing until I believe the sound

I change in a dark room

every new moon
you can feel it
the slick pink muscle
inside your mouth
and the bone of your ankle
hands spoon softness
against your forehead
your skin hums
iridescent and open

Inking

the ocean breathed
driftwood and
I watch

think of my body
a window
until the waves
reach
bring me under

soft harbour
sinking carcass
fisherman to
the soul

I hold my warm
breath and wait
with the water

Boy who cried wolf was never a goal of mine

somewhere else
I have a boy heart
and a lamb
sleeps on the
end of my bed
I go out at dusk
and stay out
the lamp-lit streets
are happy to see me
and my shadow
is just that
nothing more
the boy who
cried wolf is
my best friend
an old nightmare
a mirror
a nickname they
gave me
somewhere else
I am the wolf
and the lamb

and the bloody beating heart
and my tears
fill the streets

I bruise here

in this metaphor
unravel
my veins
after I show you
my tender heart

proof of love purple
plum myself in private
so you will think
I am pretty
even when I am in pain
I pretend
this wool is soft
not smothering

I resist the honey
pull out my
sweet tooth for you
while you refuse
to stop the bleeding
laugh at my gushing
at the wetness

my ability to overflow

I hold sensitive in one hand
and too much in the other
search my old diaries
for proof it wasn't
always like this
but it was

me sobbing on stairs
swallowing lump in throat
attempting to steady hands
fold myself into my chest

I will cry in the shower
let me wash it away
let me be clean and quiet
when I am done
I will give you my hands
see how they
do not shake

I have swallowed

so many of my own teeth

trying to avoid

an inconvenience

Cornflower blue

The pigeon died on the front steps. under the sky; cornflower blue. I do not want to make art out of it, but birth and death are a spiral and time just keeps going. I won't remember my own but maybe this is what it is like, being found and then being sick and then leaving quietly while everyone else is still inside being alive. when they remember, they gather by the door to peer and pay respects, and then someone brave buries you under the grapefruit tree in the front yard. I swallowed a small thing which is now a big thing growing inside of me, which is to say I don't want to say goodbye just yet. I want grass stains and water dishes and soft hands to touch my skin and coo with gentle voices. I want someone to give me a home.

Boxing day

in the bath, damp fingertips pulling open paperback, the permanently open window gifts me a cool breeze, and this is how I will spend the day, taking in a few words but mostly gazing at the plum bruise developing on my left knee, reminding myself every couple of minutes to deepen my forgetful breath

then my soaked body will move to the bed, curled up doom stricken, back into my day old pyjamas, not thinking about the growing growing laundry basket tucked away until it is two pm and I haven't eaten, so I place some small things between my teeth until I feel stomach settled, today my small child self is tight in my chest, is whispering, so I listen and take my cues.

I don't dance and yet

I have a
transformative experience
in this hour
between dog and wolf
and something else wanting
which is to say
I am in the
nightclub bathroom
hoping when
I go back out
the moon
will ask to kiss me
to know my flesh
translate my lips
I wash my hands
and once more
the dance floor
lifts me up

The thing I am now
After Adrienne Rich

The world tells me I am its creature. The world tells me I am its creature like I am the thing it has resulted, moulded and scraped together over the years. The world tells me I am its creature and I refuse to belong to anyone but my 3 pm shadow. The world tells me I am its creature and after 100 years of believing it, listening to the screaming of the empty winter snowfield, I become the world. Lay down in the grief of who I was to every other person, feel the ice become my bones and the thing I breathe in.

How close can you come to owning eternity?

the cost of place
is an absence of skin
dusted with pearly light

Ode in agriculture class

I daydream butterflies
imagine cowboy mountains
and 'horse girl' queerness

I wanna take these
soft grass fantasies
into myself

Summer shame

we should criminalise golf / make a pros and cons list for buying the haunted house down the street / start a petition for mangos to not have that pit / in the middle

I think we should stop denying ourselves pleasure / especially the mango eating kind / it's always summer / when I write what pleases me / in blue biro on the bottom of my shoes / press wanting to grass / lick the soles / taste dirt

i'm going to seed bomb the neighbour's front lawn / join me / i'll make burgers afterwards and drip sauce on my bare toes / you don't mind do you? / touching a mess? / this growing body / a growing list of unchecked boxes / i'll let the ants crawl up my knees

do you hate astronauts too? / their absence of touch? / tell me slowly / back porch night / shy mosquito itching / I recognise the salt of sweat / the swell of summer / from after we cut our hair off back to the mango thing / sweetness dripping down my chin / close my eyes when i take a bite / I always confuse fear / with delight / how would we do it? / remove the hard bits / the shame part? / I still blush / while I list the fruit / I want to eat

A perfect day

I woke up silent

touch toes and
drip slumber on the floor

drag me to the window
throw me to the sun

later I will rest
talk about the nights
the noise never stopped
the days of shaking earthquake legs
the feeling of cicadas in my throat

but I am older
have learnt how to bend
bodies so that when
the rain comes in the evening
I catch it all

Suburbia

I am coming home to the house by the blue. With its deep ocean and small towns. In this place, the sidewalk gum blossoms hold all, and walls spread whispers. I can go to the grocery store and see every single person I know. Coming back here is like being thirteen again, like sunburns on the tops of my feet, and knowing how to spot the tourist.

I walk up my childhood street. Past houses full of families cooking dinner, windows are oranged and glowing.

I go back to work at the pizza shop on main street and fare evade on the 784 bus home in my sleep. I know every corner and drink strawberry big M's in the back row until I am full up with street signs and sharp turns.

Back in the house, the tap drips in the downstairs bathroom, keeps me awake all night. It is my favourite song. It reminds me that this will all be the same.

Generational girlhood

my mother and my
mother's mother
live inside my belly
these hips hold my ancestors
I am awed by our creation
spiral life
bathwater baby
my being
as an ocean
grew up hand in
hand with her
and the generation of hers
pass the knife
what will I carve
into history?
find possibilities in tidepools
choose the parts that serve me
throw the rest out
bite fruit that tastes bittersweet
until I have
the whole apple
in my throat

I swallowed it
made the choice
looked in the mirror
at all of our reflections
behind me
opened my mouth
to all this contradiction

The women in my family

daughter
of saltwater women
sharp teeth and tongues

always the first to scream
name ourselves virago and
smile as we say it

us women were born in suitcases
grown beneath the orange sun
always moving on
always late to catch a flight

I am fluent in the language of searching

rising salt tides pull me back
pale moon blinds me for only a moment
forever ghosted by collapsed worlds
and stories lost to houses I came from

still, I learnt how to build a home
to collect found family
gather us all horizon lost
name this womanhood
make my own memories

sleep safely by the sea
listening to the lullaby
of salt and driftwood love

And my father

my father / gifts me laughter in the face of fear / heartbeat quickens / red cheeks / paternal lineage / things the men were taught / bird watching and / meat roasting / and not knowing how to open / a conversation with an apology / but / he asks to hold my pain for me / and the blanket on the couch / is from him / so is my bike lock / and the train timetable / and the seven calendar invites / and all the ways I know how to keep myself safe.

You are a good ocean

you are a good ocean
the kind that leaves with you
so that you can taste the salt
in the end of your hair
when you get stomach starved at night
like the time we forgot to eat all day
we were so busy searching for flowers
mom almost called the cops
when we didn't come home

you are a wish picked right out of the stars
a secret sung in the middle of the night
into the ears of two teenage girls

we owe so much to each other
the scar on my knee
the hair dyed stain in the sink
we know exactly what we need
a hand
a pull out couch
a cup of something hot and wanting

we all want someone to tell us what to do
if you say I'm special I'll believe you

Journal entry no.43

monday, 12:04pm
and I have nothing to say
so I don't

I get in the bath and
listen to the hope of tomorrow
slowly trickling upon me
slipping memories
back to sundays

around my bathroom
everything is silent
the towels on the rack
wait to meet my skin
there is soap settling into a dish
not giving up just yet
its half-melted body
on a wall
the mirror is
heavy with knowing
waiting to whisper
back my own secrets

yet nothing is actually happening
there is no new information
the birds are quiet and no one comes to call
I stay in the bath so long that
I am sure the floorboards are lonely

I am lonely too
but then I remember
that stuff always happens

even on a monday night
the moon comes out

Everyone is sad on their birthday

let's join each other
in the living room
watch tears fall
no wrapping paper or cards
instead
we bring sweet oranges and knitted wool
grieving gifts

a whole age indoors
windowpane dream state
we leant away from
breathing bodies

everyone is sad on their birthday
and in the nighttime,
we laugh for the first time all year
at the full moon
at an inside joke
between a mother
and every single night sky star

Meditations

a door is a window

is an open space

is a laugh

is a smile

is the mouth of a loved one

is coming home

is a summer storm

and a mouthful of something warm

is a dream

is a hug

is a backyard

is a secret

My practice

around my room
soft light is arriving

outside the window
morning birds are still
attempting sleep
not even the coffee smell
has begun to drift
down the stairs
but
I am about to begin

put pen on paper
blends with the noise;
jumper sleeve pushing
across page
throat clearing
neck cracks
tiny whisper
of the next line

I am alone
yet
still can't shake
anxious tics
arm jerks
stretching of eyes
hunched shoulders

it is a song
all something I can
find words for
a euphony
on the page

I sing only
to the paper

Tell me how we learn to start again

in a century or so
when the next kids come
and look at us, with wonder
they will laugh
at how we hold hands with our friends
hold parties in the grocery stores
we are 65 and have sleepovers every Sunday
take every opportunity
to hug a stranger, or to hold a hand

we know what it is like to crave touch
to hold hot skin to yours
and feel like you're unwrapping a gift
maybe they will ask us what it was like to go without
to forget the feeling of unknown breath on your cheek
to memorise bare feet on tiles, inside for months on end

and we will tell them to go outside
touch everyone, feel the electric fingertips
try to imagine a closed door,
an empty shelf and the absence of their parents' hands

I never wanted a gender anyway.

the kids are trans. they tell me their pronouns over the phone. give me eye rolls. give me space. when I pause. the kids know more than me. take my hand and pull me out into the light. into the knowing and questions and fuckery of it all. I do not want to think about myself at that age. I only want to think about their future. trans is the future. trans is whatever I want. trans is whatever you want. I want to have the answers to all of my own questions. but I can't even look in the mirror. how do you see me? what do I look like to you? the kids are too cool to be girls and boys. the limit doesn't exist now. galaxies can be identities. identities can be galaxies. you can put your pronouns on instagram now but your mum might see. I am falling in love with a boy and things are different. he makes me feel like I can be more. he makes me feel good. I want to feel good. I want the kids to think i'm cool. I tell them my pronouns. and all they do is yawn. but I am talking loud now. and I am more than one thing. I am more than my name. I refuse to see my body as any less than what it is. a magic portal. a giving thing. something cool. I am cool. I am a question. I am a kid. I am abundance.

For when I can't recognise my own face

in these hours I forget myself
numb under the fingernail moon
deep in the shadows
in the corners of my eyes
sleep is still to be wiped
in the mirror
half of me is hunting
my own kneecaps

in these moments
important questions are
to be asked, like
if I could be the frost
on the grass in the morning
could taste the crunch unseen
spirit away the need
for a recognisable face,
would I come back
into this being
arranged with a different reality?

is this it?

is this body the only one
you will know me in?
if not the grass
then what about you?
what if
nothing is fixed
and each morning
I wake up with another chance
another body
one more life

what does rebirth look like?
without raising
the kitchen scissors to your hair?
without burning down
the hard parts of yourself
in the bathroom mirror?

thank goodness for
this small magic
love letters with wet ink
to the hundred different people
I have been
and may still become

for coming home to myself
for knowing the small spaces
the shadows in the corners
of my eyes
and leaning in
letting light through
to answer the question
who are you?

A love letter to:

this queer body
and the hand-me-down haircuts
in every share house bathroom
exes who gifted me their
buzz cut bravery
and friends who brought bleach to the party
all of my black t-shirts
have orange stained reminders

to the shadowed part of my neck
lip pressed in the evenings
my hands
I stretch towards my love at dawn
hold them
close
finger print on shoulder
on lower back
on my own cheek

I only write poems about
things that scare me
so I write about my body

I feel most like a boy when
I confessed
to my housemate
I was
entering my slut era
then pressed my lips to theirs
did it so many times
we fell in love over night
and I woke up a girl again
made breakfast in bed and
left poems stuck
to our adjoining bedroom walls
until we knocked it down
pushed our mattresses together
swapped genders and
confessed our pronouns in the dark

my gender is a performance and
I haven't paid the lighting bill
you reach your hands out in the dark
and I am afraid you'll find
these hips and thighs
and name me woman

this queer body
is still becoming
is boy shorts
and bows
is pinks and no bra
tits out at the beach
is blurring it all
and growing it out
red lipstick and leg hair
op shop binder
finding new names for old feelings
transcending what I was
laughing loud
holding hands on the streets
while a blonde yells from a car that
this is not a lesbian place

this is a lesbian place

my body is a lesbian place
is a queer place
a trans place
a joy
a mess

a sacred space

my body is a murmuration
of a million tiny joy birds
working together to become
a beautiful thing in the distance
filling the sky with
something you recognise
only to take a left turn
shift
turn into something else
altogether

*I'll be a shadow of a teen girl until you tell me I
don't have to be*

a second-hand girl
lambswool pulled tight

tilt head up
to the wind
can I kiss you?

it answers
are you sure?
are you sure?
are you sure?

think about all the bad you've done
is it loud?
who loves you?
are you easy to?
the sun is proud here
and I miss my dog
and his wanting of my bigness
how I tell him to sit
and he trusts

I will come back

the teen girl inside me
forgets she's a vegetarian
I forgive her
kiss her fingers
cook her steak
and say goodbye
to the wind
and my dog
and the teen girl

I am bored
of pretending
i'm something
that can hold a mirror
uninterested in having
to decide
how to taste

I pray you take me
by the crook
skin on calling skin
ache me

somebody somewhere
is being very specific
take me there so
I forget my name
let me swallow
all this becoming

what is a girl but a dog
begging for attention
under the table?

is that enough?
is that enough?
is that enough?

After dinner

I hope
the end is light
is like
being carried
into the house
after you fall
asleep on
the drive home
you are
a little
too big
for this now

but oh

how the sound
of laughter
from next door
glows

Burnt incense

Birthdays at the shisha lounge, make my hair smell
like sweet smoke, like green apple and
licorice. When the fumes reach our heads and spin
us underneath the twinkling glass roof, we
spill out onto the field. One by one, to cleanse our
lungs. Take deep breaths of moonlight,
pressing bare legs onto damp grass. Avoid the
broken glass cigarette butts. Next, we are racing.
We run and run and run until no one can tell us to
leave. We are gone, in pairs we stride down
the main street. Keep our eyes on our toes, avoiding
gaps in the sidewalk. We buy cheap beer.
Laughing. Swallowing the last of these Fridays.

I take the number one tram to the end of the line

i'll tell you the truth then lie in my poems.
i'm numb and fucking it all up and my phone thinks i'm autistic but i'm too scared to ask my doctor about it. I wear a hat in the city and want to fight the tram drivers. they are all angry at me for not saying thank you. I am always saying I will do something and then not doing it. will that ever change? will I say it out loud and blush? I don't call people on the phone but I talk to Cush about books she has read and I agree that I should read them too. I eat a bagel and think about eye contact and she is still speaking. I am listening, I am listening and wondering what I should say next to let her know I am being a good friend. I tell her I don't know how to properly write a sentence and she laughs with her mouth open. spills her coffee on the floor. the doctor calls me on the way home to tell me my iron has gone down. I have mince waiting to be cooked in the fridge but I am too tired to cook it. I bought a book about vegetables so I can cut it up and glue it down to say something different. I took this month off work so I could work on taking care of my health but all I seem to be doing is lying in bed

and watching tv. resting, I guess but my brain likes to confuse it with depression. so does my doctor. so I am trying to write and go outside and eat more fruit and not be scared of vegetables and listen to my body but how I can I listen to it when all I can hear is.

I am trying to write and go outside and talk to people and look directly into the sun and make myself believe. that if I make something I will feel better. just like everyone else in melbourne my favourite painting in the art gallery is anguish. it's big and sad and dark. the baby sheep, and its mother and the crows make me cry and it makes me feel good to feel such big feelings but then I think about all the girls who come here to cry and I feel weird about it and it gets hot so I have to take my scarf off and leave. when I get outside I see a crow and wonder if they were just joining in because everyone else was. just like me. my funny poems are the ones that perform the best, they get accepted and shared online and sometimes an important person will pay me a hundred dollars to post it on their important website. the sad ones sit on my computer and worry my mother.

In a violet haze

pastel days
dripping like wisteria
a cloud is just a hand
cupping my cheek soft
sun rays light step ladders
on the lounge wall
dreams are expensive and yet
I loan them to you in the morning
pay tales of trapped hallways
and movie theatre screens on repeat
even my nightmares appear sun-bleached
when spilled onto bed sheets

At least I know

my love language is physical touch so I tie myself up tight
my love language is physical touch so I thumb my bruises, hard
my love language is physical touch so I kiss a stranger whose breath smells like slow rope burn
my love language is physical touch so I touch myself
my love language is physical touch so I build this body into a motel and burn it down just to keep the lights on

Love

A safe corner

I am so
full of love
I feel
as though
perhaps
I have
swallowed
the sun
or something else
very warm
like early February
at 3 pm
bleary-eyed
and sweating
through everything

watermelon
and feta
on the verandah
at my mum's house
there are
so many

things

I wish

to touch

to name

but this

love

is still

growing

so

I let it

rise

in a

shadowed space

in a safe

corner

of my kitchen

it is there

where

I become

my own

I was and then I wasn't....

in the early morning over milk, I ask you to be mine. rings of spilt coffee seeped into the table. I met you in your boyhood, fell in love with your button-ups and denim. over the months you share bouquets of secrets into my ear and I accept you for everything you are, you were and will be. we get married on the couch, in the sunroom where the bay windows play our favourite show; marmalade dusk on-demand, revolving door roommates our only witnesses. we honeymoon at the grocery store, in front of the soy milk we fantasise over a future, one that is long and loving and trans and girl and boy and neither and different every day, something that is confusing for everyone but us. I look forward to the choice, to waking up and trying something new on for the day, wearing it out and deciding it isn't for me. I take your shirt, you borrow my pronouns and we both have a newfound interest in red lipstick. maybe one day I will cut off all my hair again and beg the world to call me what it can't. boy, figment of my imagination, dream talker fantasy, blossoming again just to wilt and wake up and melt towards a different name. maybe, one day, none of this will be so important.

Eclipse

the ocean
wants so badly
to kiss the moon

the moon
pulls her in
close just enough
to taste
the seafoam salt
on her breath

they wish so much
to bruise each other
to purple the soft pinks
and make the sky blush

and yet
all they must do
is accept
the mist
and the missing
and the maddening
of the almost

The olive theory

in this new house
with a new small boy
I am wide awake
and pouring honey down my throat
hands find his hips in the dark
all of the blue unknown is in my chest
so I crawl inside
the laundry basket
it is by grief I learn what I deserve
I feel this
and that is enough
I am smiling in my dream
so I pull it closer

I don't remember my home phone number and

I hate texting
hunt me
make me
something carnal
show me my veins
teach me how I stain red
chase me towards the edge
then catch me
take my hand
and wrist
and ankle
bendable thing
all the places you
pressed your lips
so the moon will wink
with knowing
send me a message
scarred in the earth
dirt under fingernails
perpetual proof
that we have touched

You sing through the bedroom door

i.
to be loved is
to be changed by it
wool pilled and
skin tender
mercy received
in a growth state

ii.
accumulate debris and dust
egg yolk sunrises
and magpie songs
creek neighboured
we forget to recycle
and snooze our alarms

iii.
perhaps
we shall do it all
explore the stillness
take in nothing
let it silence us

we marry
one night
twin fever foreheads
touching
we decide
and that is enough

Tell me about your dream

I used to have a white rabbit
and suck the splinters

we are rich in the sun now
I watch my black cat
eat pink rose

your lower lip
hooked
on my crook
of neck

let's have a meeting
let's remember

In this sharehouse

u have
eat the rich
inked on ur arm
and I have a $50 note

I kiss
the back of ur knees
and your fever breaks
a hundred times over

hold ur face
collapse here

yes yes yes

here we are
here we want

the air leaves the room
so we can be alone

This is a funny poem

sometimes I think about
the giant abandoned strawberry
in the field in Poland

sometimes I imagine I live
right inside
and I wonder what it is like
to wake up in a rotten thing

I'll be a fruit bat baby
just for you
swing past the supermarket on the way home
to shoplift soft cheese and pink wine

I go to the beach to send an email
I go to the end of my street
just to take a picture of my face
I go to the mall but I am not American so
I'm actually just at bayside shopping centre
wandering around big w and
wondering if I am bored
enough to buy a coffee and have a panic attack

*If they ask me how I know I will tell them that
my friends taught me*

the ocean is only blue because of the sky
I am only here because I am a reflection
of everyone I have ever met
a word can mean so many different things
and still fit wrong in my mouth

it feels liberating, right?

we close our eyes
to listen to nothing

I'll tell you I miss my milk teeth
that I miss the unknowing

I was born between the street lamps
on the 11 o'clock walk home
in the silence between
the thunder clap and lightning strike
and the sound of our laugh
is where I am held

jess tells me the sun is so big
that it touches everywhere all at once
we are all just trying to carry each other home
counting bats beneath the clothesline
pointing towards the clouds

I have learnt so many things to be true
there is always someone crying
somewhere on the train
most always it is me
with someone I love by my side

I only exist for myself
but because of these people

there are so many questions
I will never even think to ask

Picture it

soon we will rejoice
rejoin and come back
to this ritual
at a friend's house
one that is full of $7 wine,
hand me down furniture
a couch saved from the side of the street
too many op-shop mugs

we will arrive slowly,
will leave the same too
with something hot in our hands and hearts
I will bring lentils, you bring sliced bread
the table is full
of heaping plates, mugs of red and
arms reaching over
around shoulders
someone will soon be kissing someone else's cheek
and everyone will be laughing at a joke

someone will put a record on
my favourite one

slowly the candles are lit
and then the moment will arrive

after our bellies are full
the kitchen table
is strewn with empty dishes
we will rise just to collapse on the couch
heads rested on the shoulders of whoever is closest
a couple dancing softly in the corner
the candles swaying and dipping in the breeze

here we are
back together again
my breath caught at the sight of it all
this shadowed gathering,
half-lit celebration of our love
of friends and food and family

I once said I didn't write love poems

I cough like a toddler
and sleep with my mouth open
asking for hope
to offer itself for breakfast
I wrote a poem in my sleep and
wake up forgotten

I want to kiss my love and
wear the proof all night
his red lipstick on my cheek

I'll ride the escalator
while you close the store
we both work full-time now
I put almonds on the shopping list
we meet again at night
the closing shift
you do the boy jobs
and I make the bed
do you want to sleep over forever?
sometimes I wake up and
find you curled in the other room

we are both still learning
how to let ourselves be held
I ask the dentist for
a mould of your teeth
so I can leave bite marks
on all the people who
opened their mouth
just to hurt you
I forgot the almonds
let's go back to the store
be so in love and
unaware that we
are blocking the isles

According to a new study

calcium is just stardust
supernovas are in our teeth
minerals found
across the universe
make up our bones
according to a new study
we owe our lives to
eggs on toast and
library cards and sweet
little treats because we
went to the doctors on our own

The work

I eat a lot of blueberries and forgive myself
my muse: the tree next to my house that just keeps
getting taller
today I lit incense, made my lunch and talked to god
put my feet on the wall
and counted the cat hairs on my socks

nothing is forever

I'm still scared of space

I venture into
new black holes
look for light switches
with only fingertips

wary of the portals
of where I close
and another life begins
of where I choose to step
up to the stars
stand in their glow

they recorded the sound
of a black hole
it sounds just like
the start of something new

I am cosmically insignificant but still so big and so deserving of love

I bought a star once
I made my own memories
danced down side streets
and reached for the moon
stopped shaving
but cut all my hair short
stayed up in the mornings
to count the bird songs
made my milk out of oats and salt
and the sound of the beach
at the end of the road
it was simple
I made the rules and made my bed
and deserved it all
I walked in the early lilac evenings
past pink houses
and dogs behind fences
went to sleep holding the sun
clutching all these things,
everything I love,
tight to my chest

Body

Today I brush my teeth

this year I named my bed home
gave in to the pull
forever hours
I sanctify my mattress
all days soften into one
and so I renaissance here

i'll paint a portrait so you can see me

I am ill and not ill enough
I am too much and then too little
I am a child who can't grow up
and a girl who is anything but

if I put a name to it does it make it real?
does it mean I have to hold it
with two hands and say hello?

I am standing at the door
bringing the night in
looking in the mirror
sick body looks back

I hold out my hand and
place it in my own
everything is quiet

I am sick because my body is
if you look close enough I am not invisible

I am documenting
I am going to the doctors
putting my feet on the dirt
asking for an answer
taking my medicine
and doing hard things
honouring my pain
I am going to the pool
and falling in love

When the fog mist clears

wrap this salt circle
around my thumb
till I bruise

again
i'm writing about a feeling

again
i'm writing about a question
I can't answer

figurine under a flood light
I thought was a woman
and what even is that
but an old dream

tell me where it hurts
sometimes it isn't obvious
how I pay
for my body
and the joy it can hold

Body work

my arms drink
the sun
sweetgum thighs
anchor to the
dirt
I blush towards
tomorrow
burning and
mortal
there is nothing else
to say
lay your arm on mine
lets not move
from here
dream out loud
of petrichor
and
know it
will come

What if I get sick?

I whisper
at what age do I
become my first fear?
no one answers
and they find nothing
in my blood
I am left in bed
negotiating with the dust
and the ache in my belly

this month
I cry in doctors' waiting rooms
more than I see my mother
memorise the reception phone number
laminated A4 signs on the wall
please wear a mask
tell the staff if you feel feverish
we don't bulk bill
check your savings account
and ask your dad to loan you $80

in the dark
I am let outside
as the moon reaches
for my cheek on the street
I give my tears to the cold
linger towards the tram

I give thanks
to the plastic chair
cupping the small of my back
catching my grief
as the doctors show
me my insides
touch me where it swells
sign the papers
grant me permission
for all this pain

the diagnoses
is not a good thing
instead a place to
point towards
and forgive

I end the night
again meeting my ghosts
in the emergency room
my eight years old and my twelve
holding my hands
whispering honey into my hurt
reminding me of the doors
we have walked out of
and will again
of the sunrise
bruised blue
like the backs of both my hands
of my someday softening

it's 3 am and this machine
won't stop telling me
I am alive

I leave the hospital and the sickness comes with me

at home,
I meet my body in the sun
in the shower
by candlelight
in the backyard
by my loves hands
I see the body as
a quilt
of sickness and light
of small
wanting to be bigger
a candle about to be lit
I teach my heart
a new song
name it rest
wrap it up and
gift it all to myself

I take my medicine in the morning
again at night
I lay down with my body
holding my ghosts hands

honey in my throat
and wake up
beside my love
apricot sunrise
I watch my heat bag
turn around
and around
and around
in the microwave

I am brave enough to take care of my body

I inhale
heartbeat searching
for an open mouth

I find altars everywhere
even in the waiting room
sun on hardwood floors
when the shadows
are breeze dancing
by the window

my name is called
and I move towards it

In sun and sickness

I believe god is in the ~~egg~~ yolk
in the cobwebs
in the collection of glass jars and
the things held inside
I play eye spy and find myself
sugarcoated in the sun
quicksanded in grief and comorbidities
this place is my bed
is also a locked door
is also an island

Pith cowboy

still with early breath

this peel scent

soars across the room

alive under fingernails

Heavyweight champion of forgetting to release the breath

I take the salt seriously
tell you I like the tongue taste
let you fossilise
my lungs in it
they have forgotten how to release
the breath anyway
february and it doesn't feel cold often here
but I can't help
searching for the melt
of my muscles
what it might feel like
to sink and stop
storm is rolling in now
so I prepare
my body
practise how I will hold it
in the mirror
let it bend in the big wind

Time well spent

i'm thinking a lot about Missy Higgins
and folding myself into cups of peppermint tea
and naps
and why every time I eat dark chocolate do I sneeze?
and learning about my own history
and what this body meant to me at 19
and how it deserves to be fed
and granting myself time
and to this being a never-ending list

An ode to my shadow

I rearrange my bouquet
devour dead bits
respect the portals
honour my pain
become friends
with my body

I give the poem time

sometimes I think i'm just writing the same poem
again   and   again   and   again

blinking towards a dimmer switch heart
deleting capital letters as I go

i'm making art about everything i've ever gone
through
carving around just to find the soft stuff

plum shades pool out of my throat and onto the
page
painting nightshade sepias with my memories

I write a poem contained in a breath
and crawl inside

You have so many parts of me to meet

if I am the stars
will you look up?
will I blind you if you see me?
can I eat the street parsley?
when my words land, are they soft?
do you have a favourite colour?
can I hold it?
can I be me?

I believe in this

this named bed day / this pull / this the body / belly
bare sunday / oil limbs / sun on myself / on almond
couch / this forever hours / and this anoint myself /
mattress / to stay all day / give it soften / here / holy

Year 24

I am a mirror
dressed in pink
curl into myself
breathe into
all four corners
of my ability
let my breath
touch
I say my name
out loud
and the timeline
begins again
it is very early
in the morning
it is very early
in my very special
life

Found objects

    1.
    2. an untouched snowfield
    3. the cool spaces
    4. my teeth, inside deep
    5. eggs cracked on a saturday
    6. the middle of a shooting star
    7. hospital gown

white walls
with the roll of my eyes
become clean
become untouched
become dust
now nothing
but blinding light

    8. fresh linen
    9. lemon laundry smell
    10. smiles
    11. a secret never heard
    12. inside of a newborn palm
    13. untouched

Incense balanced on the pizza box

the cold tap runs hot in summer
but I say thank you for the drink
say thank you for the one bedroom
cardboard boxes about to avalanche in the corner
where we scrubbed the walls for five hours
before the smell left
and we saw our future
the potential
in pinks and greens
I say thank you for
the beeswax candles in the shower
we have too much stuff
and i'm addicted to my phone
the terrible things I can hold in my hand
so I remember to say thank you
speak it into existence
orange pillows
smoke through the window
rice cooking on the stove
and my belly
my belly that can want
and then it can be fed

you bringing the bowls to bed
washing liquid
fridge that hums
sometimes this life is so terrible
I forget
that this life is so beautiful
I am here
and the sky is lilac
and you are writing a new song

Yes

marmalade sunset
I turn my head
and someone has tried
to rake the clouds
I open mouth
swallow

my face is the moon
full of love

this is not a to do list
it is a love poem

Love letter to the sun

afraid of you?
I look forward to your sight, early
flames catching the corners
melting the shadows
I meet you on the hardwood floor at four
photosynthesise silently
your orange peel persistence
confident that you will leave your mark

After

but still, I make time to lay
belly pressed down
on my sun stained carpet
myrtle thread pilling
dust smothered
warming by the hour

I am safe and
sleep softened and
turning twenty-two

Sweet dreams

My body dreams tender pink sweet potatoes with a sweet apple sauce on the side of my heart. Oh lord, I'm so glad I exist. I can't believe that I have a new big life. Every day is going to be a good thing. I'm so glad you are home. I'm so glad you are doing well and I'm feeling better now but I need you to know that I can't sleep these days and I can't write. So I'm up all night trying to stick the brightest star on the tip of my tongue. This is my soft apocalypse with one breath I become. And another I shrink into sweet milk at the bottom of the cereal bowl. For a moment I am a shiny ball of light washing dishes in the morning and getting back into bed where my body becomes soft bread and green beans. I nourish my heart with a spell that forgives. That says thank you sweet sick body for all this sweet time.

I take a breath and feel it go in cold and leave my lips warm.

I say thank you.

Special thanks

I write above all else, for my child self, who didn't have the words.

Thank you to Mum, Dad and Jessie, who pulled me through and showered me with only love. Granny who gave me stories about magic dogs and chocolate factories at the bottom of the garden.

To my love who holds my hand and listens to all my halfway poems. Everything is ok.

And to community; the queers, sickos, and poets who inspire me every day, the ones who got me on stage, the house on Davey Street that changed my life, the writing groups, and all the people who read my poems and then told me to write more. For Liv, my friend since forever.

A special thanks to the literary journals and magazines in which early versions of these poems were first published in: Plumwood Mountain Press, Verandah Journal, Bramble, Cordite, Voiceworks,

Enby Life, Suburban Review, Sunder.

Thank you to Wallea Eaglehawk and the team at Revolutionaries for giving my book a home.

Thank *you* for reading this book.